About the Author

Amanda M. Clarke is a celebrated author renowned for her insightful contributions to the field of divination and personal transformation. Her passion for writing blossomed early in life, primarily through poetry, but it was not until she navigated through a tumultuous 20-year marriage that she turned to Tarot, astrology, and angel cards. These tools not only offered her solace but also a path back to the aspirations of her youth.

Today, Amanda's daily practice of meditation and gratitude fuels her creative output. Having recognized the challenges of carrying traditional divination cards, she pioneered her unique approach by authoring divination books. These books offer the same comfort and guidance as cards but are more practical and less cumbersome, making them perfect companions for on-the-go insights and decision-making.

Amanda's love for coffee began at a young age, and this passion has percolated into her latest work, "Brewed Awakenings: Coffee-Inspired Mantras for Daily Revival." In this book, she combines her fondness for coffee with her spiritual practices, creating a quirky and whimsical guide that infuses daily coffee rituals with profound mantras. This blend of the mundane with the mystical provides readers with a delightful approach to finding daily revival and mindfulness.

Disclaimer: This Brewed Awakening book provides coffee inspired positive affirmations for daily mood setting , and it is not intended as a substitute for professional advice, diagnosis, or treatment. The information contained in this book is provided for educational and entertainment purposes only and is not meant to be taken as specific advice for individual circumstances. The author and publisher make no representations or warranties with respect to the accuracy or completeness of the contents of this book and specifically disclaim any implied warranties of merchantability or fitness for a particular purpose. The reader should always consult with a licensed professional for any specific concerns or questions. The author and publisher shall not be liable for any loss or damage caused or alleged to have been caused, directly or indirectly, by the information contained in this book. The use of this book is at the reader's sole risk

Brewed Awakenings

by Amanda Clarke

Coffee-Inspired Mantras for Daily Revival

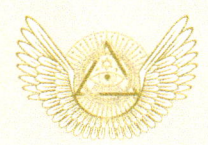

Copyright © 2024 by Koru Publishing

All rights reserved. All content, materials, and intellectual property in this book or any other platform owned by Koru Lifestylist are protected by copyright laws. This includes text, images, graphics, videos, audio, software, and any other form of content that may be produced by Koru Lifestylist.

No part of this content may be reproduced, distributed, or transmitted in any form or by any means without the prior written permission of Koru Lifestylist. This means that you cannot copy, reproduce, or use any of the content in this book for commercial or personal purposes without the express written consent of Koru Lifestylist.

Unauthorized use of any copyrighted material owned by Koru Lifestylist may result in legal action being taken against you. Koru Lifestylist reserves the right to pursue all available legal remedies against any individual or entity found to be infringing on its copyright.

In summary, Koru Publishing© 2024 holds exclusive rights to all the content produced by it, and any unauthorized use of such content will result in legal action.

Introduction

Welcome to "Brewed Awakenings: Coffee-Inspired Mantras for Daily Revival," where your coffee cup is your crystal ball and every sip is a spell! This isn't just any coffee book; it's a magic carpet ride through the world of coffee, infused with a dash of spirituality and a sprinkle of fun. Here, brewing coffee becomes a whimsical ritual, inviting the coffee-drinking spirits to dance around your kitchen.

Imagine a book where each of the 75 coffee recipes is a playful invocation, summoning the aromatic essences and weaving them with words of wisdom. As you inhale the rich bouquets of each blend, you're not just making coffee; you're meditating, floating on clouds of caffeine and calm.

"Brewed Awakenings" is your guide to turning the daily grind into a joyful jig. It's perfect for the mystic maverick, the spiritual barista, and anyone who believes that a good cup of coffee can indeed be a portal to another realm. So, grab your favorite mug and prepare to sip, savor, and be spirited away!

Caffeinated Chronicles pages at the end of this book are yours for journaling your caffeinated fueled inspirations, thoughts and creativity.

Morning Ritual

"Brewed Awakenings: Coffee-Inspired Mantras for Daily Revival," is your guide to transforming everyday coffee moments into a rejuvenating morning ritual. Here's how to immerse yourself in this unique blend of aroma and inspiration:

1. Set Your Intention: Begin by setting your intention for the day. What are you seeking—calm, clarity, energy? Hold this intention as you approach your coffee experience.

2. Choose Your Coffee: Instead of a random selection, let intuition guide you. Flip through the pages, and when you feel compelled, stop and explore the coffee and mantra that calls out to you.

3. Brew Your Coffee: Prepare your coffee in your usual way, or if you're feeling adventurous, try a new method that aligns with the coffee type selected. This book focuses on the essence and mood of coffee, without requiring specific recipes.

4. Embrace the Mantra: While your coffee is brewing, take a moment to read the accompanying mantra. Allow the words to infuse your thoughts as the coffee aroma infuses the air.

5. Mindful Enjoyment: Sip your coffee slowly, savoring each taste while contemplating the mantra. How do the flavors and the mantra enhance your intention?

6. Reflect on the Experience: After enjoying your coffee, reflect on the experience. How did the mantra resonate with your current state or mood? Consider writing down any insights or feelings that arose during your coffee ritual - you will find journaling pages to the back of this book.

7. Repeat and Explore: Use this book as often as you like—start your day with it, or turn to it when you need a midday pick-me-up. Each coffee and mantra offers a different perspective and energy.

8. Share the Spirit: Coffee and insights are best when shared. Discuss the mantras with friends or family over coffee to deepen connections and spread the warmth.

"Brewed Awakenings" offers a simple yet profound approach to enriching your daily coffee ritual. It's about more than just caffeine; it's about cultivating mindfulness, joy, and a deeper connection to your daily life. Let each cup bring you closer to the vibrant spirit within.

Salted Caramel Mocha

Recipe

Espresso, steamed milk, chocolate syrup, caramel sauce, sea salt

"May the sweet and salty waves of this mocha energize my spirit, balancing indulgence with the zest of life."

Caramel Honeycomb Latte

Recipe

Espresso, steamed milk, caramel sauce, crunchy honeycomb bits

"This delightful mix of caramel and honeycomb crunch stirs a playful joy in my day, sparking creativity and fun."

Pumpkin Cream Cold Brew

Recipe

Cold brew coffee topped with pumpkin cream foam

"The seasonal charm of pumpkin cream refreshes my perspective, reminding me to embrace change with zest and warmth."

Cafe Freddo

Recipe

Chilled, strongly brewed coffee served with ice

"This crisp Cafe Freddo sharpens my thoughts, offering a refreshing clarity that revitalizes my outlook."

Lavender Latte

Recipe

Espresso, steamed milk, lavender syrup

"The soothing aroma of lavender in this latte calms my senses, inspiring tranquility and a peaceful mind"

Chai Coffee

Recipe

Brewed coffee mixed with chai spices and a touch of milk

"The aromatic spices of chai blend with coffee to fuel my journey with warmth, spicing up my routine with adventure."

Affogato Mocha

Recipe

Espresso poured over chocolate ice cream, with a mocha sauce drizzle

"Like life's rich layers, this Affogato Mocha indulges my senses, reminding me to savor each decadent moment."

Coffee Lemonade

Recipe

Chilled coffee mixed with lemonade and served over ice

"The unexpected combination of coffee and lemonade challenges me to embrace the unusual, finding refreshment in contrast."

Sicilian Frozen Coffee

Recipe

Frozen espresso blended with almond milk, topped with whipped cream

"This Sicilian delight, cold and creamy, invigorates my taste buds and my spirit, encouraging a zest for life's sweetness."

Matcha Coffee Fusion

Recipe

Matcha green tea powder mixed with brewed coffee

"The energizing fusion of matcha and coffee fuels my creativity, blending traditions to inspire new ideas."

Scandinavian Egg Coffee

Recipe

Coffee brewed with a raw egg.

"This unique brewing method from Scandinavia reminds me to find beauty and effectiveness in unconventional approaches."

Spanish Latte

Recipe

Espresso with condensed milk and a splash of regular milk, served over ice

"The sweet, creamy Spanish Latte inspires a moment of leisure, encouraging me to savor life's sweetness amidst the rush."

Marocchino

Recipe

Espresso, cocoa powder, and frothed milk, layered in a small glass

"Like the layers of a Marocchino, may my day unfold with rich complexity and a sprinkle of sweetness."

Cortado Condensada

Recipe

Cortado with sweetened condensed milk

"The balance of strong coffee and sweet milk in this Cortado Condensada brings harmony and delight to my morning ritual."

Flat White Over Ice

Recipe

Chilled espresso with cold frothed milk

"This chilled Flat White invigorates my senses, offering a cool respite and smooth energy to fuel my day."

Cafe Miel Iced

Recipe

Iced coffee with honey, cinnamon, and a touch of nutmeg

"This refreshing twist on Cafe Miel reminds me to stay cool and collected, embracing the sweet spices of life."

Red Tie

Recipe

Thai iced tea mixed with espresso

"The exotic blend of Thai tea and robust espresso in this Red Tie excites my taste buds and broadens my world view."

Caffe Shakerato

Recipe

Espresso shaken with ice and a touch of sugar, sometimes with lemon

"This lively Shakerato shakes up my routine, sparking vibrancy and energy with every icy sip."

Espresso Tonic

Recipe

Espresso poured over tonic water and ice

"The surprising zest of this Espresso Tonic invigorates my spirit, encouraging innovation and a bubbly outlook."

Iced Vanilla Bean Coconutmilk Latte

Recipe

Espresso with coconut milk and vanilla bean syrup

"This vegan delight cools and comforts, inviting me to embrace a gentle, plant-based indulgence for a sustainable future."

Black Eye

Recipe

Drip coffee with a double shot of espresso added

"With the double strength of espresso and coffee, this Black Eye powers me through challenges with unstoppable energy."

Cafe de Olla

Recipe

Traditional Mexican coffee brewed with cinnamon and piloncillo

"This Cafe de Olla, steeped in tradition and spices, warms my soul and sparks a connection to heritage and history."

Mazagran

Recipe

Cold coffee lemonade, sometimes with rum

"Refreshing and bold, this Mazagran reminds me to embrace life's zest, mixing adventure with the clarity of lemon."

Palazzo

Recipe

Double shot espresso with ice and a splash of cream

"Cool, creamy, and brisk—this Palazzo lifts my spirits, combining luxury with a refreshing twist."

Cafe con Miel

Recipe

Coffee with honey, cinnamon, and nutmeg

"Soothing honey and warm spices in this Cafe con Miel encourage comfort and sweetness in my everyday endeavors."

Maple Latte

Recipe

Espresso with steamed milk and maple syrup

"The comforting sweetness of maple in this Latte reminds me to appreciate the rich, natural gifts of life."

Piccolo Latte

Recipe

A ristretto shot topped with warm, frothy milk in a small latte glass

"This Piccolo Latte, small yet mighty, focuses my energy, enhancing my capacity for joy and mindfulness."

Miel

Recipe

Espresso with honey, steamed milk, and a hint of cinnamon

"Each sip of this Miel infuses my day with sweetness and warmth, fostering a gentle strength within me."

Affogato al Caffe Speciale

Recipe

Espresso poured over gelato with a shot of liqueur

"This indulgent treat merges the boldness of coffee and the smoothness of gelato, inspiring delight and luxury in moderation."

Cafe Bonbon

Recipe

Layered espresso over condensed milk

"The striking layers of Cafe Bonbon symbolize life's complexities, encouraging me to delve deeper and savor each layer's richness."

Greek Frappe

Recipe

Instant coffee, water, sugar, and milk, shaken to a froth

"May the frothy vigor of this Greek Frappe stir my spirit, instilling a zest for life and a breeze of refreshment."

Shakerato

Recipe

Iced espresso shaken vigorously with a bit of sugar

"Like the lively dance of shaken ice, this Shakerato invigorates my day, sparking vitality and crisp clarity."

Ristretto

Recipe

A short shot of espresso made with the normal amount of coffee grounds but extracted with half the amount of water

"Concentrated and bold, this Ristretto focuses my intentions, empowering me to distill my thoughts into action."

White Russian (Coffee Version)

Recipe

Coffee, vodka, and cream liqueur

"Let the rich, spirited blend of coffee and cream liqueur smooth my evening with comfort and a touch of indulgence."

Kopi Tubruk

Recipe

Indonesian-style coffee where coffee grounds are boiled along with a lump of sugar

"May the boldness of Kopi Tubruk remind me to embrace the robust, unfiltered experiences of life."

Egg Coffee

Recipe

Vietnamese coffee with egg yolks whipped with sugar and condensed milk

"This creamy, luxurious Egg Coffee nourishes my soul, blending tradition and richness into each sip."

Borgia

Recipe

Espresso with hot chocolate, whipped cream, and orange zest

"The dynamic zest of orange, the depth of chocolate, and the boldness of espresso inspire creativity and zest for life."

Cafe Zorro

Recipe

Double espresso diluted to a regular coffee strength with hot water

"In the strength and simplicity of this Cafe Zorro, I find clarity and the courage to face the day unadorned"

Long Black

Recipe

Similar to an Americano, but with the espresso poured over hot water

"This Long Black stretches out the day's possibilities, inviting me to savor each moment as it unfolds."

Dirty Chai

Recipe

Chai tea latte mixed with a shot of espresso

"The spicy melody of chai and the robust touch of espresso bring adventure and energy, spurring me on to face new challenges."

Peppermint Mocha

Recipe

Espresso, steamed milk, chocolate syrup, peppermint flavoring

"Let the invigorating peppermint and rich chocolate remind me to find joy and renewal in each season's turn."

Affogato al Caffe

Recipe

Vanilla gelato drowned with a shot of hot espresso

"This fusion of hot and cold invites me to appreciate the beautiful contrasts in life, finding harmony in diversity."

Espresso Romano

Recipe

Espresso served with a slice of lemon

"May the zesty lemon and bold espresso invigorate my senses, encouraging a fresh perspective on the day ahead"

Caffe Breve

Recipe

Espresso with half-and-half instead of milk

"As creamy as the clouds and as rich as the earth, this caffe breve comforts and grounds me simultaneously."

Bulletproof Coffee

Recipe

Coffee blended with butter and coconut oil

"Empowered by this blend, I charge forward with sustained energy, ready to meet challenges head-on."

Vietnamese Iced Coffee

Recipe

Strong brew with sweetened condensed milk, served over ice

"The sweet strength of this coffee awakens my spirit, infusing me with vitality and the zest of a new adventure."

Cortadito

Recipe

Espresso with a splash of steamed milk, similar to a cortado

"Let the strength of espresso and the softness of milk balance my day, blending resilience with comfort."

Cafe Melange

Recipe

Coffee with whipped cream and sometimes a shot of brandy

"This melange, rich and spirited, inspires a cozy warmth, stirring thoughts of comfort and creativity."

Galão

Recipe

Portuguese drink with espresso and foamed milk in a tall glass

"In this tall glass of relaxation, I find the lightness to rise above daily troubles, sipping clarity and calm."

Cafe con Leche

Recipe

Strong coffee mixed with scalded milk in a 1:1 ratio

"With every sip of this harmonious blend, I am reminded of life's simple pleasures, fostering peace and joy within."

Dalgona Coffee

Recipe

Whipped mix of instant coffee, sugar, and hot water, served over milk

"This frothy top above smooth milk lifts my spirits, reminding me that joy can be whipped up from simple ingredients."

Cafe au Lait

Recipe

Equal parts brewed coffee and steamed milk

"As I savor this café au lait, may it soothe my soul, blending serenity with each sip, harmonizing my day."

Iced Latte

Recipe

1 shot espresso with chilled milk over ice

"This iced latte cools my thoughts, bringing clarity and refreshment, empowering me to flow through the day with ease."

Pumpkin Spice Latte

Recipe

Espresso, steamed milk, pumpkin pie spice, and whipped cream

"Let the seasonal spices of this latte inspire a celebration of change, igniting a cozy, creative spark within me."

Espresso Con Panna

Recipe

1 shot espresso topped with whipped cream

"With the boldness of espresso and the sweetness of cream, I embrace a balanced approach to tackle today's endeavors."

Honey Almond milk Flat White

Recipe

Espresso mixed with honey and almond milk

"As sweet as honey and as smooth as almond milk, this drink reminds me to embrace life's sweetness with health and vigor."

Caramel Macchiato

Recipe

Vanilla syrup, milk, espresso, and caramel drizzle

"The swirling layers of caramel and coffee energize my spirit, crafting a delicious narrative of sweetness and strength."

Cafe Bombon

Recipe

Equal parts espresso and condensed milk

"This rich blend of strong espresso and sweet milk serves as a decadent reminder of life's dualities and richness."

Affogato

Recipe

1 shot espresso poured over a scoop of vanilla ice cream

"As the espresso meets ice cream, I am reminded of life's sweet and intense moments, balancing pleasure with energy."

Cortado

Recipe

Equal parts espresso and steamed milk

"In this balance of strength and softness, I find my equilibrium, ready to face the world with poise and resilience."

Cold Brew

Recipe

Coarsely ground coffee steeped in cold water for 12-24 hours

"This cold brew refreshes my spirit, offering a cool, deep dive into a pool of tranquility and renewed vigor."

Turkish Coffee

Recipe

Finely ground coffee brewed with sugar and cardamom in a cezve

"May the rich heritage of this Turkish coffee connect me to ancient wisdom, inspiring introspection and cultural appreciation."

Nitro Coffee

Recipe

Cold brew coffee
infused with nitrogen

"Like the cascading
bubbles of this nitro
coffee, let my thoughts
rise briskly, bubbling
with creativity and new
ideas."

Vienna Coffee

Recipe

2 shots espresso topped with whipped cream

"This indulgent blend of strong espresso and soft cream inspires a luxurious pause, a moment of comfort and sophistication."

Red Eye

Recipe

1 shot espresso added to a cup of regular coffee

"With the robust combination of coffee and espresso, I am fueled with unstoppable energy, ready to take on long challenges."

Frappé

Recipe

Blended ice with coffee, milk, sugar, and flavored syrup

"This frappé whirls me into a playful dance of flavors, light-hearted and free, swirling with delight and spontaneity."

Espresso

Recipe

1 shot of espresso

"With each sip, I awaken my senses and ignite my spirit, ready to conquer the day with vigor and clarity."

Cappuccino

Recipe

1 shot espresso, steamed milk, milk foam

"Let the frothy delight of this cappuccino bring joy and lightness to my heart, soothing and uplifting me."

Americano

Recipe

1 shot espresso, hot water

"As I drink this Americano, I embrace the simplicity of life, feeling grounded and deeply connected to my surroundings."

Latte

Recipe

1 shot espresso, steamed milk

"This latte nurtures my soul, offering warmth and comfort, encouraging thoughts of peace and contentment."

Mocha

Recipe

1 shot espresso, steamed milk, chocolate syrup

"May the rich blend of chocolate and coffee fill me with warmth and sweetness, inspiring happiness and creativity."

Flat White

Recipe

1 shot espresso, steamed milk (less foam)

"I let the smooth and creamy texture guide me to a place of calm and focus, where every challenge is manageable."

Macchiato

Recipe

1 shot espresso, a dollop of foam

"This macchiato sharpens my focus, cutting through the noise of the day to reveal clarity and purpose."

Irish Coffee

Recipe

1 shot espresso, whiskey, sugar, cream

"Let the spirited kick of whiskey and the boldness of coffee empower me, invigorating my mind and stirring my soul."

Almond Joy Latte

Recipe

Espresso with coconut and almond syrup, topped with whipped cream

"Like the candy that inspires it, this Almond Joy Latte reminds me to find joy and indulgence in the small, sweet moments."

Rose Vanilla Latte

Recipe

Espresso with rose water and vanilla syrup, steamed milk

"The delicate flavors of rose and vanilla in this latte encourage me to embrace elegance and tranquility in every sip."

Hazelnut Mocha

Recipe

Espresso mixed with chocolate and hazelnut syrup, steamed milk

"This Hazelnut Mocha wraps me in warmth, inviting a cozy comfort that energizes and nurtures my spirit."

Cardamom Black Coffee

Recipe

Brewed coffee with cardamom pods

"The exotic hint of cardamom in this coffee broadens my horizons, spicing my morning with anticipation and zest."

Coconut Cream Latte

Recipe

Espresso with coconut milk and a splash of cream, topped with shaved coconut

"This tropical Coconut Cream Latte transports me to serene beaches, inspiring calm and a break from the everyday rush."

Espresso Martini

Recipe

Espresso shaken with vodka and coffee liqueur

"This spirited Espresso Martini shakes up my evening, blending sophistication with a buzz of excitement."

Maple Cinnamon Latte

Recipe

Espresso with maple syrup and a sprinkle of cinnamon, steamed milk

"Every sip of this Maple Cinnamon Latte fills me with warmth, wrapping my senses in a sweet, spicy embrace."

Smoked Butterscotch Latte

Recipe

Espresso with smoked butterscotch sauce, steamed milk

"The rich, smoky sweetness of this latte stirs a sense of comfort and nostalgia, igniting warm memories and new dreams."

Orange Mocha

Recipe

Espresso with chocolate and a hint of orange zest, steamed milk

"This vibrant blend of orange and chocolate in my mocha brightens my day, sparking creativity and a zest for life."

Mint Coffee

Recipe

Brewed coffee with fresh mint leaves or mint syrup

"The refreshing essence of mint in this coffee rejuvenates my spirit, reminding me to breathe deeply and renew."

Caffeinated Chronicals

Daily Sips of Insight

Daily Sips of Insight

Daily Sips of Insight

Daily Sips of Insight

Daily Sips of Insight

Daily Sips of Insight

Daily Sips of Insight

Daily Sips of Insight

Daily Sips of Insight

Daily Sips of Insight

Daily Sips of Insight

Daily Sips of Insight

Daily Sips of Insight

Daily Sips of Insight

Daily Sips of Insight

Daily Sips of Insight

Daily Sips of Insight

Daily Sips of Insight

Daily Sips of Insight

Daily Sips of Insight

Daily Sips of Insight

The "Daily Guidance" series offers an innovative approach to finding spiritual wisdom and practical advice. Each book in the series is a unique tool designed for daily introspection and decision-making. Readers are invited to meditate on a question or seek general guidance for the day, then flip to a random page in the book. The page they land on provides a personalized message from various spiritual sources, such as angels, tarot, or spirit animals. With each turn of the page, these books deliver insightful, positive messages and mantras to inspire personal growth and provide clarity on life's daily challenges and decisions.

Other books in this series:-
Daily Angel Tarot Reading
Mystic Tarot Cat
Oracle of the Tarot Cat
Vibes Unveiled
Spirit Animal Oracle
Answers from the Oracles
Messages from the Angels

More on the Bookshelves at www.korupublishing.com

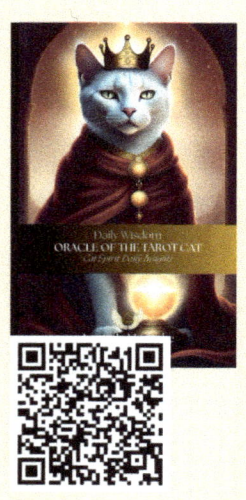